Anthony the Chicken's Adventures

Anthony the Chicken's Adventures

BOOK II

CAROL TURNER

ReadersMagnet, LLC

Anthony the Chicken's Adventures: Book II
Copyright © 2022 by Carol Turner

Published in the United States of America
ISBN Paperback: 978-1-956780-89-5
ISBN eBook: 978-1-956780-90-1

All rights reserved. No part of this publication may be reproduced, stored in a retrieval system or transmitted in any way by any means, electronic, mechanical, photocopy, recording or otherwise without the prior permission of the author except as provided by USA copyright law.

The opinions expressed by the author are not necessarily those of ReadersMagnet, LLC.

ReadersMagnet, LLC
10620 Treena Street, Suite 230 | San Diego, California, 92131 USA
1.619.354.2643 | www.readersmagnet.com

Book design copyright © 2022 by ReadersMagnet, LLC. All rights reserved.
Cover design by Ericka Obando
Interior design by Mary Mae Romero
Illustrated by Jebb Impok

ANTHONY THE CHICKEN MEETS DEUCE

Anthony the Chicken had ridden on a train. He'd been to the Kansas Oil Museum and learned how to dig for oil. At least how they drilled for oil in the 1920's and 1930's. Anthony was sure he was ready for another adventure. It was almost the end of spring, Anthony and Bugger were going to make sure Dick the refrigerator would be alright during the winter. Bugger added more straw beneath the refrigerator to keep him warmer, Anthony helped. That winter had come and gone, it was spring again. Anthony had itchy feet. He'd learned years before that he would have to make his own adventure. Anthony waved good-bye to Bugger the farm dog, and walked down the dirt and gravel driveway. He looked up and there were tall hedges on both sides, the taller trees made the driveway a lot shadier. It was as if Anthony was walking under an arbor.

Bugger called, "See you later, have fun on your new adventure! I'll visit Dick often to make sure he's okay."

"Thanks for doing that," Anthony turned and answered, "I knew I could count on you. See you later, you're a good friend."

"Have a wonderful time and be safe. You're my best friend," said Bugger.

Anthony reached the end of the driveway. He looked to his right and saw a medium-sized dog walking on the road.

"Hey, you want some company to walk with?" yelled Anthony to the dog. 'I think I've found my adventure,' thought Anthony.

The dog stopped walking and turned around, Anthony the Chicken ran to catch up to him.

He said, "Can I join you? You going anywhere in particular? My name's Anthony."

"Nope just walking, my name's Deuce," said the dog, "Oh I've heard of you," Deuce looked Anthony up and down, "you really are a chicken."

"Maybe just a chicken but I'm a chicken looking for an adventure."

"Have you found one yet?"

"Maybe talking to you will become my next adventure," said Anthony.

"Me! Don't adventures need to be something new and exciting," exclaimed Deuce, "that doesn't sound like me."

"You're different," answered Anthony, "I've never seen a black dog walking down the road before. That's exciting."

Deuce looked around, he saw nothing but pastures and trees. The only hint of modem technology were the telephone lines. They must be in the country. The quiet was deafening. Deuce looked at Anthony the Chicken, he enjoyed Anthony's company. The walk would be boring and lonely all by himself.

Deuce looked at Anthony and said, "I do know a lot of stories."

"You do! Well I want to hear one," said Anthony.

"Are you sure," asked Deuce.

"Sure, listening to a story would make the time go by faster. Tell me about how you came to the home where you are now."

"Now there's a story," Deuce said with a big smile.

"Tell me," said Anthony.

"I remember it like it was yesterday. A day that began badly for me ended up turning out great. I went to live with Wayne and Carol," said Deuce as he began his story. "I saw Wayne come into the store, he looked like a man with a purpose. I made Wayne notice me by barking and barking from my box. Even though I was in a box with my brothers and sister I barked and smiled my best smile. Wayne finally noticed me, he picked me up and then I 'puppy-hugged' him. I kissed him as only a puppy can," Deuce continued. "At the same time Wayne knew I was meant to be with him, he carried me out to his car. Wayne stepped inside and held me up high. Wayne said, "This is the one, I can tell." I kissed him a lot, Carol asked if we needed to buy anything from the store. She pulled from the parking lot, driving and trying to keep her eyes on the road.

"No we're fine," Wayne said, "I already know what I'm going to name him...Deuce-Armistead II, after Armistead, we'll call him Deuce. Two, the 2nd, get it?"

"Yeah I get it," said Carol.

Deuce added, "She didn't seem to sure about me but she came around soon."

Anthony listened carefully as he and Deuce walked along the road. Anthony looked over his shoulder, he saw how far away the farmhouse was.

He said, "Remember Deuce how far we walk forward is how far we have to walk back."

"Well then Anthony," said Deuce, "let's sit down on the grass underneath those trees."

"Good idea," said Anthony, "you're a good storyteller. I could listen to you all day."

"Thanks," said Deuce.

Anthony found a soft, grassy spot under a tree and motioned to Deuce to sit there.

"Anthony this is a wonderful spot. I'm glad you chose it," said Deuce as he looked around.

"Thanks Deuce, sitting here makes me hungry," said Anthony as he looked around he picked up some bugs off the ground to eat.

"There's a conversation starter," said Deuce, "we're under these trees. Tell me Anthony what's your favorite food?"

"That's easy," said Anthony, "I love sunflower seeds! Kay and Palmer eat them all the time at the farm. Then they drop the shells on the ground What about you?"

"Well I'll eat just about anything," Deuce continued, "I suppose my favorites are baby carrots and bread and butter pickles."

"That's quite a combination," said Anthony smiling.

"Oh you don't eat them together," Deuce laughed, "Carol gave me baby carrots as training treats. In the backyard she would throw my squirrel toy. I'd run after it and when I returned it she gave me a baby carrot. It didn't work very well, I just wanted to play 'keep-it'."

"What's keep-it," asked Anthony.

"That's a game where Carol would throw the toy then I would keep it. She thought I would pick up the toy and bring it to her. I wouldn't, I'd just dart back and forth as I brought it closer and closer to her. Carol would play tug-of war with me. She would try to get the squirrel toy from me. It wasn't shaped like a squirrel she just called it that. After we played she'd give me a baby carrot anyway because I was a good dog."

Anthony laughed and smiled, "So you've told me about baby carrots, now tell me about the pickles."

"Oh that's when Carol would comb me for fleas."

"Really," said Anthony as he scooted away. He certainly didn't want fleas hopping onto his feathers.

Deuce saw Anthony move and quickly said, "I don't have them now. If you see me scratch it's because I have dry skin. I need to drink more water to keep my skin softer I guess. I don't always remember to drink as much as I should. That's probably why Wayne put that small plastic pool in the backyard. You know one of those blue plastic toddler pools."

Anthony nodded.

"Wayne would clean it out and fill it with fresh water every week. Unless it rained, then it got dirty, or froze. I hated that. When it was too hot Carol or Wayne added ice to the pool or I could go into the house to cool off. My house was a place outside under the kitchen part of the house, it was good-sized and it had a concrete floor. During the winter Wayne spread an old rug section on the floor then he put straw on top of that. He also had a light rigged up in there so I would be warm if it was cold outside."

"WOW, he did a lot for you," said Anthony.

"Yes he did," answered Deuce, "he was my best buddy. He always called me his 'hound-dog'."

"What about the bread and butter pickles," asked Anthony.

"Carol would comb me with a flea comb about once a week in the winter and every night in the summer. I always knew when she was going to do it, she'd say, you want some pickles? Then we'd go into the kitchen I'd watch as she put pickles and pickle juice in a container. In another container she put dish soap, warm water and the flea comb. Carol would then carry them to a low table in the living room. She would lay some papers on the table and ask me to lay down. I watched her every move but I kept my eyes on the pickles. When I would lay down on the floor at the end of the table she'd give me a pickle. She'd comb me with a mixture of dish soap and water, it felt good. I learned quickly that whenever I did what she said she gave me a pickle. They were good. Sometimes she found fleas sometimes she didn't. Carol and Wayne gave me pickles at other times too. Mostly when they needed me to do something. I do love those pickles, I would do almost anything for them? Only pickle slices though, don't give me a whole pickle or another kind. Just bread and butter pickle slices."

They got up to walk on down the road until they came to another shady spot.

"So you've told me wonderful stories about baby carrots and pickles," said Anthony. He pointed with his feather to the new shady spot and the trees where they sat down again.

"Now tell me about your adventures, Anthony," said Deuce.

"Well," said Anthony, "I walked to see the ocean, I rode on a train part of the way."

"You did? I always thought trains moved to fast to do that," said Deuce surprised.

"I'd exercised my legs for about a year before I left. I did lots of walking stretching my leg muscles to build them up. Actually the train was standing still when I jumped on. I still did do a lot of walking though."

"Did you do this by yourself?"

"Oh no," laughed Anthony, then he smiled, "I met other chickens along the way, Robert, Louise, Bertie and Ruth. I even met the Purple Pasha and Meep a teenage dinosaur."

"What," asked Deuce completely surprised. He'd never heard of a Purple Pasha, he thought dinosaurs were extinct, they weren't alive anymore. "Meep, what a name, a teenage dinosaur?"

"Yes," answered Anthony, "I was walking to the ocean and I was walking through the desert. It was really hot. Far ahead I saw something purple on ground. I thought I was seeing things and in the middle of the road sat a man all dressed in purple. As I got closer I heard some sort of humming sound."

"Why was he purple?" asked Deuce.

"I'm getting there," said Anthony.

"Sorry for interrupting," said Deuce.

"Thanks I'll go on," said Anthony, "the man looked purple because he only wore purple clothes, shoes, shirt, pants, socks, jacket everything was purple. The humming noise I'd heard was the Purple Pasha repeating 'ohm' over and over, he called it his mantra. He said it helped him to center himself to find peace, whatever that means. Come on let's walk and talk," said Anthony.

Deuce got up to walk some more. "When did you see the teenage dinosaur?"

"That was the next day," said Anthony.

"Okay, this really happened? I want to hear about the dinosaur." Now Deuce sat back down on the cool grass by the side of the road looking up at Anthony. He was ready to listen.

"The next day the Purple Pasha and I woke up. We both heard a noise...meep...meep in the distance. We looked at each other neither of us had heard a noise like that before. We packed up our campsite, I just had a bed roll, the Purple Pasha didn't have anything. We walked slowly in the direction of the noise. As we kept walking the 'meep' got louder and louder, we knew we were close. We kept walking until we came to a cliff. At the bottom was an orange glow, we'd never seen that before."

Deuce's eyes got wider and wider. 'This is a great story,' he thought.

Anthony went on, "As our eyes got used to the orange glow we saw that the glow was coming from a small dinosaur. The dinosaur didn't seem mean, only scared. Both the Purple Pasha and I talked gently to the small dinosaur, we used baby talk to coax the dinosaur to climb up. The dinosaur kept saying 'meep…meep…meep' again and again. Finally the dinosaur climbed up to us saying 'meep' the whole way. The baby dinosaur reached the top and the first thing he did was hug the Purple Pasha, he hugged me too. The Purple Pasha reached into the pocket of his wide, purple pants, found some rope for a leash. (Yes it was purple) He easily placed the leash on the dinosaur and named him Meep. Meep glowed the whole time we walked. Getting to sleep that night was a challenge because of the glow! Meep fell asleep immediately but I had to finally put a blanket over Meep so we could sleep. The next morning Meep was gone! The Purple Pasha was awake and had taken Meep for his morning potty break. The Purple Pasha wanted to take Meep back to his family. He left that morning while I went on to the ocean."

"What happened to Meep?" asked Deuce anxiously.

"The Purple Pasha said he was going to take Meep back to his family. He thought maybe that's why Meep was so scared. I've always wondered what happened to Meep, if he got home and he's okay," Anthony wondered partly to himself.

"That was some story," said Deuce, then he got up and walked over to the trees. He ate some leaves from the bottom.

"To experience it was amazing," said Anthony he also watched Deuce. He asked, "Deuce why are you eating leaves?"

"Sometimes I like it, sometimes everything doesn't come out the way it should. Like I said sometimes I just like the taste like salad."

"I see, but I didn't need all that other information," frowned Anthony.

"Sorry, Carol's Dad was a doctor so I heard her say how she felt frankly. Guess I borrowed that," said Deuce.

"Let's move on, you got any more stories? I'd love to hear them," said Anthony.

"Okay just give me a minute. This shade does feel good, just sitting here and talking."

"I agree with you, I'll wait. It's just nice to sit here quietly," said Anthony.

"Let's walk, it's wonderful weather and I just want to get to my home," Deuce said as he slowly stood up.

"That's a good idea my feet feel rested. Do you know how to get home from here?"

"Yeah, I'll know it when I see it, I just need to follow this road," said Deuce.

Anthony and Deuce walked a long way down the gravel road. There was no need to talk just enjoy each others company as they walked. Anthony thought the silence was very comforting. Anthony looked up seeing the clouds and the blue skies. He watched Deuce and the dog walked straight ahead as if he had a purpose. Like he had someplace he needed to be.

"Well Deuce are you going to share any more stories?" asked Anthony.

"I'll try to make mine as good as the one about Meep the dinosaur," answered Deuce.

"I'm sure that any story you tell will be interesting," said Anthony.

"Maybe I'll blend a couple together to make one good one," laughed Deuce.

Anthony smiled and laughed as well as a chicken can.

Deuce started his story, "When I first moved into the house a cat already lived there. If I remember correctly his name was Peachnik. I heard Carol tell Wayne the children she worked with had named him. It was a combination of the names Peaches and Nicky."

Deuce continued, "One night Wayne opened the back door to let me in like always. I ran in and suddenly Peachnik out of no where hit me in the face. It didn't hurt, it was just a playful hit. I quickly turned around I was ready to roughhouse. I didn't see the cat anywhere. I got down on my elbows with my front paws while my back paws stayed up high, my tail was wagging! I looked to my right and left, I still didn't see Peachnik! Then I felt him hit me again, another playful one. I looked up and there he was sitting on a dining room chair. So when I walked by Peachnik had hit me, TWICE! In a flash he jumped on my back, he didn't dig in his claws. I started running across the room with Peachnik riding on my back like a cowboy on a horse. Wayne had called Carol to come into the room."

Carol watched us run around the room. "Thanks for calling me Wayne. This is priceless."

Peachnik finally jumped down then we started 'play-fighting'. I remember Carol said we tusseled like brothers. Wayne said we were so lucky they got along so well. Peachnik would jump on me and I would roll over. We rolled around a few times. We never hurt each other when we wrestled, we just enjoyed it, It always ended when I slapped Peachnik back. I guess I didn't know my own strength. I think I hit Peachnik to hard. I should've remembered that but we were having so much fun. Whenever Peachnik came into the back yard I would watch. Peachnik didn't even pay attention to me. I'd take a drink of water and go on into my house," Deuce's eyes filled with water as he remembered.

"I'll bet that's a comforting memory to have," said Anthony.

"Yes it is," said Deuce.

"Were there a lot of cats in your house?" asked Anthony.

"Always. I think Wayne was a dog person and Carol was a cat person. Wayne liked cats and Carol liked dogs but not as much. All the cats that came later just tolerated me," answered Deuce.

"Another favorite memory or story was whenever Wayne would take me flying," continued Deuce, "he called it flying actually I rode in the passenger seat in his truck. Wayne would open the door for me and I would jump in onto the seat. Wayne got in on the driver's seat. Deuce looked at Anthony, "it's good he didn't expect me to drive. I don't know how. I must admit I did like sitting in the driver's seat. We always went out to the country near our town. Especially if it was nice weather. There was always a particular house Wayne would drive by, that's where my dog buddies lived. There were three dogs that ran to their chain link fence. They would bark 'hello, hello' to me so I would start barking 'hello, hello' back to them. All of us barked 'hello, hello' to each other until Wayne passed the house. Most often the window was rolled down, us dogs could hear each other real well. After he drove a bit Wayne would pull the truck to the side of the road and stop. He'd say 'stay hound dog' then he jumped out to cut some flowers for Carol. He'd get back in the car and lay the flowers next to the seat, they always smelled nice. I'd try not to sit on them as I looked out the window, The breeze felt so good on my face. I put my front paws on the window's edge. I'm sure there are some claw scratches on the front door from where I'd get so excited. It was an accident, I didn't mean to. We passed some open fields. I would hear Wayne tell me to look at some turkey or deer on one side but I always looked on the wrong side. I missed them every time, almost. Wayne had to keep reminding me to not jump out of the car, I really wanted to catch them. When I saw the cows I really wanted to be with them. I'd probably scare them but they did seem so laid back. When the weather was bad we didn't go flying or just on a paved road to take a short trip. The best part was spending time with Wayne. When we got home he'd type on the computer while I laid down on the floor next to his chair. I liked being near the door to the room. If anyone came in I'd be the first to see who it was."

"So you watched over him," agreed Anthony smiling.

Deuce nodded, "Anthony why are you laughing?"

"That must've been fun Deuce. I can see you hanging out the window."

Deuce began to remember another part of his life. He stopped walking and sat down in the middle of the road. Deuce looked away in the distance. Anthony knew the dog was thinking about another tale to tell. Anthony sat down to listen. The chicken looked up at the dog.

Deuce started saying, "It seemed everyday when Carol came home from work she walked from the garage up the brick sidewalk to the back door. I always made sure to be sitting on the sidewalk. Sometimes I'd be laying on the grass in the sun. I'd lift my head to nod hello with my eyes partly open. Then Carol would lean over and pat my belly. She always said 'My Deuce, I bet you're warm laying here in the sun.' She said that every day but I never got tired of hearing it. If I was sitting on the sidewalk she'd pat my head and rub my belly saying, 'My Deuce.' The she'd go inside. After supper," Deuce continued, "Wayne or Carol would open the door to call me to come inside. When I got older there would be a puzzle with treats inside for me. I had so much fun finding those treats. When Wayne was younger he'd play with me on the floor. Sometimes he'd throw a toy so I'd catch it or find it and bring it back to him.

Deuce looked at Anthony, "I'd play fetch inside."

"Other times Wayne would put a part of the toy in his mouth. Both of us would growl and shake our heads. That game would always tire me out. Then I would jump on the couch to sit and relax with Carol. When I was a puppy Carol would always let me rest with her on the couch. Sometimes she would lay me on her lap and rub my tummy until I'd fall asleep. As I got older and bigger Carol and Wayne got a new couch. I couldn't get on that one. I had my own chair though, no one got on that chair except me. The chair was next to a window, whenever anyone came on the porch I barked really loud. When the mail came I barked sometimes I growled. Wayne and Carol always knew when the mail had arrived."

There was a long silence until Anthony said, "That was a wonderful story Deuce."

"It's true. Every word," said Deuce softly.

"Oh I'm sure," said Anthony, "You're lucky, I'm not let inside the farmhouse. Palmer and Kay are very kind except I couldn't go inside. I would've liked to though."

"We still have a ways to walk Anthony," said Deuce, "it's your turn to tell a story."

"Where are we going Deuce? Is it much farther?"

"I'm not sure, I'll know it when I see it."

"Well I did meet this turtle named Tim," said Anthony.

"A turtle?" asked Deuce.

"Oh yes he lived in a place called Topia. His name was Tim."

"Is he still alive?" asked Deuce.

"As far as I know he is," answered Anthony, "I first saw Tim dancing with other turtles. They were singing to the Great Theodore. I didn't know Tim then."

"Who's the Great Theodore?" asked Deuce.

"The best I can tell you is the Great Theodore is someone the turtles admire and look to for guidance," answered Anthony.

"Is he their god?"

"I'm not sure Deuce. Anyway I slept up on a bed of pine needles. I was tired after a long walk. I heard singing. I discovered the turtles dancing in a circle. They saw me and stopped right away. Tim yelled at me to halt so of course I did. In a polite way he asked who I was, if he could help me. He asked me to join him and all the turtles for lunch. The turtles cooked their potatoes outdoors in a stone oven. Each turtle picked a potato from a basket, poked a couple holes in it, then put it in the oven. I poked holes in my potatoes with my beak, they had never seen that before."

Anthony continued, "I told him about the turtles I seen on the farm they didn't dance or sing but they liked water. Tim told me there was a pond nearby. We walked there and surprise! All of the turtles were already there sitting in the water around the edge of the pond. Now chickens don't like water but by this time I had stuck my toes in the ocean. Tim told me some more then he swam to a log. He climbed up on that log to sun himself."

Deuce liked that story.

"I almost forgot," said Anthony, "the stone oven was tall with two oven doors. There were steps leading to the upper door. I didn't get close enough to tell if the steps were made from sticks or stones."

"Like a ladder, huh," said Deuce.

"Not really, just little steps sticking out of the stone for the turtles to climb up to put food in the upper oven."

"There were others I met on my way to the ocean. I met a Dorking chicken named Bertie. He had five toes. Roberta, excuse me, Robert was an ISA Brown chicken he saw the ocean with me."

"What's an ISA chicken? I've never heard of that," asked Deuce.

"An ISA Brown chicken is intelligent and calm. Another name for an ISA Brown is a backyard chicken because they live in people's backyards."

Deuce nodded, he thought, "I've always lived in Wayne and Carol's backyard, why would I live anywhere else?"

ANTHONY THE CHICKEN'S ADVENTURES: BOOK II

Anthony looked ahead down the road. There was a covered bridge. Like the one on the outskirts of Pettigrew. Footsteps echoed because of the roof and the sides. The sounds had no place to go. Anthony looked up towards the sky, across the bridge was a beautiful rainbow. It formed a wonderful arch over the top of the bridge. Anthony remembered that he'd heard there was gold at the end of the rainbow. Deuce saw the bridge and he was so happy. He started to run, gradually he began running faster.

'Maybe Deuce is after the gold too,' thought Anthony. So he began running to the bridge.

Deuce reached the bridge first. He sat down, looked over his shoulder. He saw Anthony running to the bridge.

"Stop Anthony, you can't go across," yelled Deuce. He put out a paw to stop Anthony.

"But Deuce, why not?" asked Anthony as he slowed down to a walk.

Deuce explained the best he could to Anthony, "This is the Rainbow bridge, I'm the only one who can cross."

"Deuce what about Wayne and Carol? I thought you were going to see them."

"No Anthony not yet. I'll see them some day. I liked your stories. Now I'll get to meet the first Armistead."

"I'll miss you Deuce. Now I have to walk by myself."

"I'll see you later Anthony, good-bye," Deuce waved with his tail, "you'll meet someone to walk with I know you will."

"I liked your stories too, bye Deuce, thanks for being my friend," Anthony waved good-bye with his feathers.

Deuce waved again with his tail and walked slowly but happily onto the Rainbow Bridge.

ANTHONY THE CHICKEN LEADS FRIENDS TO THE GROTTO

Anthony The Chicken had walked Deuce to the Rainbow Bridge. Anthony was sure there was gold at the end of the rainbow. Maybe he'll find it next time.

He thought, "Maybe it just wasn't my time to find it." He shrugged his shoulders. Anthony looked up as he walked, there was the farmhouse. Bugger was there so was Kay and Palmer. He had missed all of them.

He saw Dick in the near pasture and waved to him. Anthony remembered Dick couldn't see that so he yelled.

Anthony raised his voice and said, "Hello Dick, I'm back." He saw the V-handle smile, he'd heard him.

As Anthony walked closer to the driveway to the house he noticed a red, black and brown 'bump' in the road. It was moving!

"Oh no", Anthony said to himself, 'not another dog,' he got closer, 'not another chicken.' He paused and closed his eyes part-way trying to see better. Anthony saw that the 'bump' had feathers but it was the biggest chicken he'd ever seen.

As she moved, Drucilla the turkey looked anxiously to her left and right. She looked down to a small furry worm crawling next to her and said, "Melvin, what are we going to do? It's not safe for me to walk in the middle of the road,"

"I'm not sure, I don't know," answered Melvin in a deep voice.

"But what about that dinosaur I saw! It could be following me!"

"Drucilla, you didn't see a dinosaur!"

"Yes I did! It was big and brown! I had to walk to the other side of the road so it wouldn't see me." she said.

Melvin stopped and looked up to Drucilla. "What you saw was a thresher that had been left out in the weather. It was in a field and you thought you would be safer on the other side of the road but it wasn't a dinosaur. It was some kind of farm machinery"

"Well it could've been a dinosaur," said Drucilla.

Melvin just shook his head from side to side, Drucilla will believe what she wants to.

By this time Anthony the Chicken had realized that the 'bump' was a turkey. He wondered why the turkey was talking to the ground?

"Hello I'm Anthony the Chicken, is there something I can help you with," he asked politely.

Drucilla stopped, her eyes got wide, she said nervously, "I'm Drucilla, and that's Melvin the furry worm," she pointed to the ground.

Then Anthony saw the furry worm on the ground, "Hi Drucilla," Anthony knocked down, "Hi Melvin," Anthony always thought worms were delicious but here was a talking one.

"Does anyone live in that house?" asked Melvin.

"Yes, Kay and Palmer, Bugger the farm dog too. They are all very nice. Bugger is a very good friend, he's a three-legged dog."

"So they're your friends," asked Drucilla, she sounded worried.

"They're fine, they won't hurt you," said Anthony. He raised one feather to hopefully help Drucilla feel better.

All three of them started walking and reached the end of the driveway. Melvin and Anthony were ready to keep on walking to the chicken coop but Drucilla was still worried and looked all around.

Bugger was walking around in the back yard. Every now and then he looked down to sniffed the grass. Bugger looked up and saw the three of them.

He took one look at Anthony and he barked, "Hello!"

Bugger started to run toward Anthony and Drucilla, he hadn't seen Melvin yet. Frightened Drucilla ran and hid among the hedges. Anthony was so happy to see Bugger he'd forgotten the others were even there. As Bugger ran closer he suddenly heard a loud voice from the ground.

"Don't come near my friend!" yelled Melvin.

Bugger stopped in his tracks, he'd never heard a voice that loud. He noticed where it came from, he looked down and then he saw Melvin. "Why you're just a little furry worm. Where did the turkey go?" he said as he sat down.

"She went to hide from you behind the bushes. I mean every word I said," said Melvin in a firm voice.

Anthony saw the confused look on Bugger's face. Quickly he said, "Bugger these are my new friends," he pointed with his wings, "This is Melvin the furry worm, you've met him Drucilla the turkey is over there behind the hedge."

Bugger felt better so he stood up and said, "It's good to see you Anthony. I've missed you. I'm glad you're safe."

"So am I Bugger, my three-legged friend. It's great to be home. I invited to Drucilla and Melvin to stay here awhile."

"That's fine. Drucilla's the turkey right? She can stay with you in the chicken house," said Bugger.

"Drucilla is trying to hide and stay undercover. She thinks people are trying to hurt her. We need to think of someplace safe."

Both Anthony and Bugger thought and thought. Melvin watched them while Drucilla stayed behind the hedge.

After a few minutes Bugger sat down and said, "Oh, the grotto would be perfect!"

"Yes, the grotto! Why didn't I think of that," exclaimed Anthony.

"What's the grotto," asked Drucilla. She slowly cam out from behind the hedge.

"Yes, where's the grotto? Is it safe," asked Melvin.

"It's a great place not far from here," said Anthony, "We can just go back down this road and around the comer. A little bit down that road and it's a place with three smooth, large rocks. The trees grow over it like a canopy. It's really shady and cool but the sun comes through a little. No one would know you were there. The grotto would be perfect for you."

"Will there be room for Melvin?" asked Drucilla. She wanted to be sure she and her friend could be together. Melvin was small but he listened carefully and appeared to nod.

"Oh sure, there's plenty of room for both of you," said Bugger.

All of them started down the road together. Anthony the Chicken, Drucilla the turkey, Melvin the furry worm and Bugger the farm dog walked side by side together. As Melvin wiggled along he struggled to keep up with everyone.

Drucilla stopped, turned around and said, "Melvin be sure to stay in the shade." Things seemed to have changed and now Drucilla was watching out for Melvin.

Melvin answered, "Right." He moved to slide between the small rocks.

Anthony and Bugger watched Melvin move to the stones.

Drucilla looked at Anthony and Bugger saying, "Worms need to stay out of the sun, they can only be in the sun a short time."

"I didn't know that," said Anthony, 'What will happen?'

"They'll dry up and die," said Drucilla firmly as she walked.

"She has to remind me to stay in the shade but I look out for her," said Melvin.

Both Anthony and Bugger said, "We'll be watchful too."

They walked a little way and then Drucilla stopped and pointed with her wing, "What is that little building? It looks like a little house! Who lives there? I thought you said no one was here," she sounded scared again.

Bugger tried to comfort Drucilla saying, "No one lives there, it's empty."

There was a small white building in the middle of the field. There were tall windows on each side and a door on one side. All the windows had planks of wood on them and door was closed. There was a chimney on the roof. Anthony and Bugger stopped next to Drucilla, Melvin was careful to stop in the shade of a weed. There were hardly any cars or trucks in the road very often so they knew they were safe.

"I've heard that it used to be a corn crib and before that it was a schoolhouse. I'm not sure what Palmer uses it for now," said Anthony, "do you know Bugger?"

"He probably uses it to store stuff," said Bugger.

The four began walking again. Drucilla turned around and reminded Melvin often to stay in the shade.

Melvin frowned at being told what to do like a child but she was right. "I'll remember," he said.

They arrived at the comer of the road, there was another road leading to the left. That was another gravel road, at the bottom of the hill Drucilla and Melvin saw more shade, the two also saw what looked like a small creek.

Drucilla looked down the road they were on, she saw a large two-story house. "Who lives there?" she pointed.

The animals looked at Bugger, he answered, "no one but a relative of Palmer's stores some stuff there."

"Can we see it before we go to the grotto?" asked Drucilla.

"Sure," said Anthony "Now I remember when there was a Halloween party there. Kay spent a long time getting the house ready. There's no furniture and a small gazebo in back."

"There's no real path to the house we'll need to make our own."

"That's alright," said Drucilla. She and Melvin climbed through the boards of a fence and were already walking to the house.

"Drucilla seems to be getting braver by the minute," whispered Anthony.

Bugger nodded. He and Anthony pushed themselves through the boards on the fence. They looked as Drucilla

walked faster, then Melvin had to wiggle faster remembering to stay in the shade.

Drucilla walked to the front of the house, Melvin, Bugger and Anthony followed her. When they arrived at the house Drucilla walked through the doorway, there was no door. It was leaning against the wall. Drucilla eagerly climbed up the stairs, they rest remained downstairs to look around.

"This is the kind of house that Drucilla likes," said Melvin.

Anthony the Chicken noticed there was no kitchen, Bugger saw that too. He suddenly felt hungry, "Where would anyone have eaten?" he asked.

Melvin saw, in what he supposed was the living room, many trunks and clear, plastic boxes. It was dirty and he could see that many critters had been there. He wiggled all around the boxes, each one had letters and numbers on them. He could hear Drucilla coming down the stairs so did Anthony and Bugger.

"There's only two rooms upstairs, you should see the wallpaper," she said, "Those were most likely the bedrooms, the rooms are so big, so there were several beds in each."

"WOW! I wish I knew who lived here," said Anthony.

"Me too," said Drucilla, "but I'm sure it was a family with children. Let's go see the gazebo!"

"Good idea," said Bugger "I don't think I've ever seen that."

Anthony went outside to the back, Drucilla followed close behind.

"I'll bet the family ate some meals out here when the weather was nice," said Bugger.

"I'm sure they did this is a nice place. The weeds have overgrown though," added Melvin when he caught up with the others. Since he had no legs he moved slower.

"It's getting late and we've got a long walk to the grotto," said Bugger.

"That's true," agreed Anthony.

"Let's go, the house will be here a long time," said Drucilla.

When they got to the grotto Anthony the Chicken took a look at his image in the creek. His lucky hat was still on his head with the feather. He felt it on his head and he felt so much better inside.

While Anthony was looking in the water, Drucilla saw a small, tasty snack in the sun on a rock. Melvin saw it too. Drucilla watched the snack it was a small caterpillar. As Drucilla moved slowly closer she was able to see the thin stripes of yellow, black and green on the bug.

Drucilla moved closer to sniff the caterpillar. When she did the caterpillar turned it's head and said, "Hey! My name's Peggy and you're in my sun! I was just trying to keep warm!"

Drucilla was surprised she jumped back, Melvin heard the voice too, he jumped backwards. Bugger and Anthony looked at each other then they looked in the direction of the rock. They both had heard something but neither one were sure what it was.

Drucilla wasn't sure what to think she'd never heard a snack speak before. She said, "Are you alright? Who are you?"

Peggy answered, "I'm Peggy, I'm fine, thanks for asking," Melvin thought she didn't sound like she was fine.

Drucilla took a few steps back saying, "I'm sorry I was in your sun. Won't you get too hot?"

"No, I'd gotten wet from the creek so I thought I'd dry off in the sun. If I get to hot I'll move."

"Of course," said Melvin. He'd never heard a caterpillar talk before.

Anthony looked around saying, "Well this is the grotto and the trees give you enough shade. The rocks will keep you cool, they're big enough to sit on! Bugger and I will be at the farmhouse down the road to the left. Have a good night and stay safe."

As Anthony and Bugger turned to leave he looked around the area, he was sure he'd heard a noise. Bugger and Anthony were walking back to the farmhouse. Anthony looked up, noticing it was early evening he was glad that Drucilla and Melvin were safely at the grotto. Anthony and Bugger were pretty sure that no one was really hunting for Drucilla.

The next morning at the farm Anthony put on his lucky hat and walked over to the doghouse.

"Good morning Bugger," said Anthony leaning into the doorway. Bugger moved around but he was still asleep. "Good morning Bugger," said Anthony a little louder.

"Oh hi," said Bugger, "going to the grotto?"

"Hello," smiled Anthony, "let's go to the grotto to see how Drucilla and Melvin spent the night."

"Sure but let me wake up some more," said Bugger as he yawned.

"Sure," said Anthony, he walked around thinking that Bugger sure took a long time to wake up.

After awhile when Bugger was more awake Anthony and Bugger walked together down the dirt and gravel road. When they got to the grotto they saw Melvin pulling grass and leaves to Drucilla for breakfast. She sat up while she rubbed her eyes with her wings.

"Morning," said Melvin after he put down the leaves and grass.

"Anthony, Bugger it's good to see you," said Drucilla. "By the way Melvin did you get any bugs? Where's that caterpillar?"

"Not sure, all I know is that after Peggy dried off she went into the grass. I never saw her again. No bugs this morning just leaves and grass, sorry."

"How was last night? We hope everything was alright," said Anthony.

"Well," said Drucilla, "we met Peggy...no bugs Melvin? I sure like my protein in the morning."

Melvin wiggled away to look for bugs. Bugger watched the worm so he followed, "Can I help?" he said.

"Who's Peggy?" asked Anthony.

"She was a caterpillar we saw here on this rock," said Drucilla then she added, "you understand how chickens and turkeys like bugs."

Anthony nodded, his mouth began to water.

"Anyway then she talked!"

"Really!"

"Yes Peggy said she was getting some sun on the rock."

"Bugger and I thought we'd heard something when we left," said Anthony.

At that minute Bugger and Melvin returned. Melvin had found some bugs for Drucilla. After all he wanted to make sure she ate, behind him he pulled a large leaf that had bugs on it. Drucilla and Anthony looked up.

"Here's your bugs Drucilla on the leaf," said Melvin.

"I helped," added Bugger.

"Looks like there's enough bugs for both of us Anthony," said Drucilla.

"Thanks, maybe just one, at least it's not dog food," said Anthony remembering Gene the rat and the trailer.

After breakfast Drucilla and Anthony laid on the smooth, large, cool rocks looking at the clouds. Anthony watched a spider web reaching between two branches. A leaf was suspended in the middle of the long strand. A breeze caused the leaf to spin around and around. Anthony wished he could ride around and around, like that merry-go-round at the museum. Anthony closed his eyes and though how warm the sun felt. Bugger laid in the shade so did Melvin. Melvin knew he shouldn't lay on a flat rock in the sun so in case the sun started to shine on the rock Melvin moved. He laid safely under a small bush to relax but he remained alert for Drucilla in case she needed anything.

Bugger looked at the clouds as he lay in the shade. He saw that one cloud looked like a dog, next to it one looked like a bone, behind that one that looked like bacon! Bugger thought, "I feel hungry! I always feel hungry! I'd better start thinking about something else."

Drucilla thought about how good it felt to just relax, to not be afraid, not need to be somewhere. She saw a cloud that was the shape of the house, she was sure there were other shapes if she looked long enough.

Everyone closed their eyes thinking about how wonderful it was to lay there.

Anthony looked at Bugger. He must be having a dream, as Anthony watched, his three legs seemed to be running in place. "Whatever he's chasing he's moving fast," said Anthony to himself. He looked at Drucilla, her feathers were arranged neatly in a circle around her, of course Melvin was stretched out napping nearby. It was nice to be the only one awake.

The trees provided enough shade to keep the large, flat rocks cool. The sun sparkled through the leaves to keep his friends warm as they slept. That's why Drucilla, Bugger and Melvin slept so well. Anthony sat up, he'd thought he'd heard something, he looked at the sky it was sort of a 'blue glass jar' color. Anthony had seen a lot of blue glass jars lining the shelves at the farmhouse. Anthony moved his feathers up under his head. He leaned back on them enjoying his 'alone time'. He rested that way for a long time.

When the sprinkling began everyone felt the raindrops on their eyes. They opened their eyes rubbed them and blinked. The rain continued to fall faster. The friends quickly stood up and ran under the trees. Then each one began picking the leaves off the branches, they began weaving them together to create leaf umbrellas. These simple umbrellas would keep them dry until they reached the farmhouse and shelter. While they were working Peggy the caterpillar scurried under the bushes when it started to rain. She continued to watch and smiled knowing that no one knew she had been watching. She had carefully watched until she was sure all of them were asleep. Peggy quietly and carefully tiptoed to where they were. Peggy looked around then she moved closer to Bugger, she'd never seen a three-legged dog before. Peggy walked all around Bugger looking at him.

Melvin jumped up and rode on Drucilla's back. Anthony and Bugger were ready to run back to the farmhouse in the rain. Suddenly as quickly as it started the shower stopped!

'It must've been a short, spring shower,' thought Anthony. He looked up and the sky was clear, the clouds were like fluffy marshmallows. Drucilla, Melvin and Bugger came from beneath the trees looking at the sky. All of them began walking towards the farmhouse.

As they walked Anthony looked at the soybean field, he saw something orange! He walked across the road to the fence, he climbed through the boards. Anthony could still see something orange, it was near the ground. Anthony the Chicken used his feathers to push apart the soybean plants, he saw pumpkins growing on the ground.

Bugger noticed Anthony looking in the field. He walked over to Anthony, he asked, "What do you see Anthony?"

"Something orange, pumpkins I think," answered Anthony. He was still looking at the field.

Drucilla and Melvin saw Anthony and Bugger by the fence. They went over to Bugger to see what interested Anthony. Melvin was riding on Drucilla's back so where ever she went he had to go.

"Oh," said Bugger "so that's where they planted them."

Anthony asked, "I thought they only grew soybeans and corn?"

"It used to be that way Anthony. Last year, I think, Kay wanted to try growing pumpkins to sell. I heard Palmer say he'd try growing then using one acre."

"Did Kay want to make pies or try to grow a giant pumpkin?" asked Drucilla.

Bugger grinned and said "I don't think so but Kay does make good pies."

By this time Drucilla had walked to where Anthony and Bugger were. Since Melvin was on Drucilla's back he was higher and he could see better.

"I see pumpkins!" said Melvin, he turned to look at his back. Melvin wanted to see if the hair on his back had gotten wet.

"That's what I thought Melvin," said Anthony.

"I wonder," said Drucilla, "if I could make pies with them."

"I suppose you could try," said Melvin.

Anthony nodded. Bugger was remembering the many leftover pumpkin pies he'd eaten. There were always plenty of leftovers at holiday time.

Suddenly Melvin, the furry worm, turned away from the group and looked down the road. He climbed down from Drucilla's back. They were near the farm. Melvin was the first to hear the noise. He looked down the road, then they came over the hill, the noise got louder and louder.

"Look," yelled Anthony, as he pointed with his wing.

Everyone came to the road.

"Here they come, Look at that," said Drucilla.

"I've never seen anything like it," said Bugger.

"Me either," said Melvin as he nodded.

They were marching in rows of six. As they marched the grasshoppers chanted "Too...too..to-wee" Maybe the strange chant helped the grasshoppers to stay in step. As they marched they looked straight ahead they seemed to be hypnotized.

Usually Drucilla and Anthony would think of the grasshoppers as delicious snacks but these grasshoppers were different. Bugger wondered if he'd been in the sun to long without a hat. Melvin just saw some friends, fellow bugs.

"Too..too...to-wee." the grasshoppers marched right by them. They looked straight ahead as they marched they didn't even seem to notice them. When they moved by the group just stood next to the road watching them with surprise.

To everyone's surprise Melvin got in line with them, he wiggled along behind them. Anthony and Bugger watched him march away.

"He'll be back," said Drucilla.

Anthony, Bugger and Drucilla slowly walked behind the grasshoppers and Melvin following them. They followed at a distance so they wouldn't be mistaken as being a part of the marchers. Soon the marching grasshoppers turned down the road towards the grotto. Melvin scooted right along with them. By this time Anthony, Bugger and Drucilla were curious so they followed too.

"That's our grotto," said Anthony, "Where are they going?"

"Let's find out," said Bugger.

"That's why we're following them isn't it? What's got into Melvin? He seems to be in a trance," said Drucilla.

The three friends stopped on the grass near the creek still watching the grasshoppers and Melvin. What they saw the insects do next surprised them even more. One by one each grasshopper stopped marching and went to a nearby tree. Each one pulled off a leaf, walked to the creek and laid the leaf on top of the water. Melvin also pulled a leaf off a tree and laid it on the water. The three friends didn't say anything they just stared. As each grasshopper placed the leaf on the water the insect climbed on top of the leaf, like a raft, and floated down the creek. There was a mild breeze in the air that helped to push the leaf along. Melvin followed the grasshoppers. He also floated down the creek on a leaf raft.

Drucilla watched Melvin float away, "He'll be back. I'm sure of it," she said.

Anthony and Bugger wondered if she was right as Melvin floated down the creek. That was the last time any of them saw him.

After they watched Melvin they walked slowly back towards the farmhouse.

Drucilla said between tears, "What'll I do without Melvin? Who's going to keep him out of the sun?"

Anthony said gently, "I'm sure he'll be fine. Melvin will remember to stay in the shade. You taught him well." He patted Drucilla on the back with her wing.

Bugger agreed adding, "You taught him well, Drucilla."

"Come here Drucilla back to the farmhouse. You can spend the night in the chicken coop."

"Thanks Anthony," said Drucilla.

The three friends walked up the dirt and gravel driveway. Bugger went directly to his doghouse. Anthony and Drucilla walked to the chicken coop, there silently Anthony made his nest as Drucilla laid down on the the straw floor.

The next morning Anthony and Bugger ate breakfast. They looked up and saw Drucilla.

"Morning Drucilla," greeted Anthony, "Let's go see how the pumpkins are."

"No not now, I'm sure they're fine," said Drucilla, "I'll go ahead and start on down the road. Maybe I'll see Melvin!"

Bugger added, "Yeah! Or maybe you'll see another furry worm!"

"You'll never forget Melvin," said Anthony, "perhaps you'll find a new friend."

"Maybe I will," said Drucilla. She started walking down the road. Occasionally while she walked Drucilla would look down by her side hoping Melvin would be there. She never saw Melvin but she missed him.

As Anthony and Bugger watched Drucilla each one thought they saw a thin yellow leaf on the ground. Anthony the Chicken took a few steps forward and looked closer. It was a furry yellow worm! It was trying to catch up to Drucilla! At that moment both Anthony and Bugger knew that Drucilla was going to be alright.

ANTHONY DRILLS FOR OIL (SORTA)

Anthony the Chicken had seen the ocean, met chickens from different parts of the world. He'd met Gene the Rat, Dick the Refrigerator, Tim the Turtle, and he'd learned about the Great Theodore. Anthony's favorite memory was of helping and teaching Bugger the farm dog how to walk again. Doing all these things had helped Anthony the Chicken to learn a lot about himself. He realized he was a lot stronger than he thought, more capable too. Anthony was a curious chicken, he wanted to find out more about the world around him. Anthony wasn't sure what he would do next or what kind of adventure he would have.

"Perhaps I just need to find my own adventure," Anthony thought.

He had ridden on a train on his way to see the ocean. At the time he had saved himself a few steps, at the time he'd also had a chance to rest his feet. Anthony had noticed that on the east side of his town of Pettigrew there were some railroad tracks where a train would pass by. Surely the train would take him to an adventure. Anthony decided he would be there the next time it passed by waiting for it.

A few days passed while Anthony waited then a small train passed by. It had an open car. The train slowed down a little more and stopped. Anthony trotted next to the car, caught up to the doors and hopped on. He checked to make sure his lucky hat with the feather in it was still on. Anthony was sure glad he'd exercised his legs with all that walking.

"WOW! That was harder than I expected," he looked around the inside of the train car, "I need to find a place to rest," said Anthony out of breath.

Anthony looked around some more and pulled out a large box then he saw an old burlap sack. It was dirty but it would be fine Anthony folded the sack with his feathers. That dirty, burlap sack provided him a soft place to rest his feet He leaned against the box and relaxed as the train gathered more speed. Anthony watched through the open door of the train car as the trees seem to passed by.

The train began to slow down Anthony suddenly woke up. "I must've fallen asleep," said Anthony blinking his eyes. He looked outside then blinked his eyes again. Anthony said to himself, "This place looks nice, when the train slows down some more I can jump off and take a look." He looked around to see if anyone was listening. Good no one was around. The train slowed to a pause not a stop. Anthony saw a small group of houses. He jumped out of the train car, he rolled once when he hit the ground. He sat up, shook himself to get off any dirt, He saw a schoolhouse and a cabin. There was a large grassy area it was shaded with lots of trees. He also saw a few picnic tables. Anthony stood up and walked away from the tracks. He came to a metal chain link fence. Anthony looked up at the fence, climbed it sticking a foot in each chain. Sort of like climbing a ladder. He strolled on the grass towards the small white schoolhouse.

There was a bell on a pole next to the building. A concrete step at the front door, a sidewalk led away from the schoolhouse. The more Anthony looked around, on the other side of the building he saw an old-fashioned wooden merry-go-round. The kind a child would sit on and ride.

"Now that could be fun," thought Anthony.

He got closer to the merry-go-round and looked around on the ground for a long branch. Anthony finally saw one, picked it up and used it to hoist himself up and onto the merry-go-round. When he got on the wooden seat he straddled it the best he could. He used the branch like an oar in the water, he poked one end into the ground to push himself around and around in circles. As he rode around he saw a small green bridge over a dry grass gully. He also saw a small brown house. The merry-go-round slowed to a stop, Anthony jumped off. He walked over to the door of the schoolhouse. He stood on the top of a nearby rock so he could reach the doorknob. Anthony wanted to see what the inside looked like.

Slowly Anthony opened the door. He saw so many interesting things. Anthony knew what he wanted to see first. He looked at at the front of the room next to the chalkboard was a piano. There were many student desks and a large teacher's desk near the piano. Anthony also saw a big black stove used to keep the room warm in the winter. The chicken looked a the piano, he knew what that was because Kay and Palmer had one at the farm. On cool summer or spring nights when the windows were open Anthony could hear the wonderful music coming from the piano. He wanted to create beautiful music too. He jumped onto the piano bench then on up to the keyboard. His feathers were so light that some of them slipped between the black and white keys.

"I need to put more weight on the keys," said Anthony.

So Anthony jumped onto the keys with his feet, he ran up and down the keyboard making high sounds and very low sounds. But no beautiful music just noise. A lot of terrible noise.

'How did Kay get all that wonderful music from the piano at the farmhouse? What did she do?' he wondered. Anthony looked again and he was certain the two pianos were the same size and shape. He jumped down onto the bench and looked back at the piano.

Then he saw the bookshelf. Anthony had only known how to read for a few years. He'd learned his ABC's and read everything he could find on the farm. Whenever he had a chance to practice his new-found skill he took it. He jumped onto the floor from the piano bench and walked over to the medium-sized bookshelf. It had only two small shelves with glass doors. There were quite a few books on the shelves.

There were spelling books, arithmetic books, story books and even a geography book.

'What would a geography book be about?' he thought. He opened the book and saw a lot of maps. Anthony made a face and put it back on the shelf.

Anthony picked out the next book. It was an 8th grade reader but the words seem to difficult for him to read. There were a lot of 4th grade readers, maybe they would be easier. There were many stories, 'The Elephant', 'The Pet Faun'.

'What's a faun? I know what an elephant is,' wondered Anthony.

There were poems too, 'The Snowman', Anthony smiled he knew what a snowman was. After all he'd seen snow he lived in the Midwest.

He looked up and saw all the desks. Anthony counted them, he was better at reading than counting. He slowly counted 27 desks, almost all of them were different sizes. On the wall, up high, behind the teacher's desk was a picture or painting of a man in a dark suit. He had gray hair, it looked like it was pulled back. Anthony thought he didn't look very happy.

'At least he could have smiled,' thought Anthony.

Anthony walked to the front door of the schoolhouse. He opened it and went down the sidewalk. To one side he saw a cabin and he walked on across the bridge. Then Anthony heard a creak as if something needed oil. He looked up to find the noise and he saw a windmill.

'There's one on the farm in Pettigrew,' thought Anthony 'but it didn't move that much, It's very windy here.'

Creak! Creak! Anthony looked to another side. He saw a large brown building labeled Wash House. There was another small gray building next to it. Anthony saw a small brown

house. He walked down the sidewalk that lead to it. As he got closer to it he saw there was a window on the top of the door. On the window Anthony read, 'The Magnolia Petroleum Company Field Office'

'So it's not a house. That's where I need to go! Maybe I can learn to dig for oil here,' he thought.

He started to open the door, he looked up, Anthony saw that evening was coming. He knew that now was the time to find a place to spend the night.

Anthony looked around, almost all the houses had porches. He knew he wanted to be up off the ground. Anthony wished he'd remembered to bring a bedroll on this adventure. The porch on the Wash House was the highest off the ground. Anthony decided that porch would be the safest place to stay. Anthony the Chicken began collecting dry grass and leaves to make a nest. Louise had taught him how when he was on his way to see The Ocean. He picked up a 'featherful' of grass and leaves. He climbed up the steps to the porch several times depositing his 'nest' on there. On his last trip Anthony saw a piece of fabric on the ground.

'H-m-m-m I didn't see that before it would make a nice blanket.' thought Anthony.

He picked it up with his beak, he shook his head from left to right to shake out any bugs or dirt from it. It was big enough to make a fine blankets Anthony carried the fabric in his beak to the nest he'd created on the porch. While he was arranging the grass and leaves into a nest he noticed something move out of the comer of his eye. He looked up and saw a raccoon walk across the grass.

"Hey, I'm Anthony the Chicken! Haven't I seen you somewhere before?" hollered Anthony. He was remembering what Dick the refrigerator had said about critters.

The raccoon began to run then he stopped and turned around. "Not me, but were you by a lot of refrigerators?" asked the raccoon.

"Yes," said Anthony.

"Oh then you probably met my cousin Ralph. He said he sleeps on refrigerator shelves at night. My name's Rex it's hard to tell the difference between raccoons,' said Rex.

"Then I did see Ralph, you and Ralph do look the same, are you twins?"

"No, I see you're sleeping on the porch. I'm headed to a picnic table, I might find a late night snack there, in case someone dropped their food. Also under the table I'm protected in case it rains," said Rex, "Sleep well, be careful there's a cat that roams around here. She's black and white I think, I don't know her name."

"Thanks for telling me. I'll sleep with one eye open, good night," said Anthony.

He watched Rex walk to the picnic tables. It was kind of early to go to sleep. After he made his nest he thought he'd walk around. He remembered Dick had said that a critter came at night and slept on his shelf. Then the raccoon he and Bugger had seen was Ralph, Rex's cousin. Rex seemed nice. As Anthony walked around he did keep his eyes out for the cat. Cats don't like chickens and a chicken is very much like a bird. Next to the Wash House was another gray house. Next to that house was a wooden sidewalk, then in a row there were signs that read Doctor's Office, a Print Shop and at the end of the boardwalk was a Grocery Store. All of those were in that long building. He also saw some giant metal things that looked like giant grasshoppers. Anthony looked at them a long time, they never moved. He walked past the windmill, all the houses, everything was surrounded by a chain link fence.

'Since it's getting dark I'll look at more tomorrow,' thought Anthony.

As he walked back to the Wash House he heard the dry leaves crackle under his feet. Anthony heard another sound, he walked faster. If that noise was the cat Anthony wanted to be safe in his nest. He didn't like cats! He got up on the porch to his nest. He took off his hat and laid it nearby, Anthony slept soundly that night. He figured he would look inside the Wash House tomorrow. The next morning he woke up on the porch, put his hat on, he noticed that Rex was gone.

Anthony opened the Wash House door, he stepped inside. The first thing he saw on the wall was a black and white cut-out of a picture. It was a woman smiling as she did her laundry. To his right were two washing machines. He walked over to them, one was blue. There was a sign that read that both of them were from the 1930's. Anthony saw more pictures on the wall. There were copies of laundry soap ads and a picture of a child cranking an old washing machine. There was another picture of a woman hanging out her laundry to dry. Anthony saw more washing machines on the other side of the room. There was a really old one that looked like the one the child was cranking in the picture. He followed the rug down the hallway to two tall doors. One had a sign saying 'Men' and the other had a sign saying 'Women'.

"Well this is a bathroom!" said Anthony out loud.

There was another door at the end of the hallway that led outside. Anthony looked and saw a long ramp that led down to the side of the Wash House to the sidewalk. Anthony walked back down the hallway, past the washing machines. He went out the front door onto the porch down the steps to the sidewalk. He saw the little brown house and he also saw the small gray house.

'I haven't seen that one,' thought Anthony.

When Anthony reached the sidewalk he stopped and looked back at the Wash House. He shook his head from side to side.

"Only humans would need a separate building outside to go to the bathroom. A chicken can go anywhere," said Anthony.

He looked again at the small gray house. He looked and it seemed the same as the other gray houses. Anthony jumped up the steps to the porch to look inside anyway. He saw a piece of plastic paper nailed to the wall of the house by the front door. It had words on it. Anthony jumped onto a chair on the porch to read the words.

Anthony read, 'This house was built in 1918...it was right here in El Dorado,' Anthony finished reading the paper and jumped off the chair thinking, 'I'm glad I learned to read. A chicken can find out a lot of interesting things.'

Anthony noticed that the front door was open. 'Well, that's unusual.' he said to himself. So he walked right on in.

There next to the door was a soft looking double bed. Anthony jumped onto the bed, it was soft so Anthony jumped and jumped. He'd always wanted to do that. There was a pretty silk pillow leaning against the bed pillows. It was a old-fashioned iron bed. There was also a small lamp clipped to the head of the bed. As he looked around the room he saw a birdcage with no bird. He would keep watch for it. There was a bucket with a lid on it under the bed.

'Why keep a bucket under there?' thought Anthony.

He saw a sewing machine on the other side of the room. He knew that Kay had one in the farmhouse but he didn't think it looked like that one. He walked on to the back room. There was a refrigerator in one corner but it wasn't blue like Dick and not as tall. The table was set and there was a stove. On the shelf was a bowl of kitchen tools, he also saw a long clear tube.

'It seems hollow, I wonder how it was used,' thought Anthony.

He looked around some more and everywhere it seemed he saw empty jars on shelves sitting in a row. He also saw that the back door was open.

"Whoever left the front door open that must be how the bird got out," said Anthony to himself. "this place is awfully small to have been two apartments, that's what the paper said."

Anthony was about to go out the back door when he saw a small table by the door. He jumped onto the step outside the back door. Anthony saw a large, freshly planted garden. Rows were dug in the dirt and big rocks lined the edges.

'At least in Grandma's house things were sort of real. I couldn't cook on that stove and the refrigerator wasn't cold though,' thought Anthony.

Anthony walked to the front of the house and walked straight to the little brown house. He was still worried about Rex though, he hadn't seen him. Anthony walked over to the two picnic tables. Under one there was a small circle in the grass that was where Rex had slept. Anthony had wanted to ask Rex about The Magnolia Petroleum Company but Rex was gone. Anthony hadn't seen the cat anywhere. He walked on up the sidewalk and opened the door. No one was there, everyone was gone.

'Maybe they're out digging for oil,' thought Anthony.

He went inside and there were three big desks in the front. In front of the desks was a long fence-like barrier that stretched from one wall to the other, on the top of it was a long flat board. In the middle was a clear plastic piece of paper with words on it. Anthony flew to the top of the barrier. He read the plastic sheet of paper and read that the landman who worked here was responsible for getting permission from the land owners to dig on their land.

"Well that makes sense to me," said Anthony to an empty office.

He looked around the office, he saw land maps, a couple telescopes and a pair of boots.

Anthony saw the boots and thought, 'I suppose the landman has to walk in all sorts of places.'

He went out the back door onto a small deck. On it were two small crudely built wooden chairs between the chairs was a small table, also crudely built. Anthony sat on one of the chairs to think. He was thinking about those big metal grasshoppers. There were at least six of them. He'd only seen small green or brown grasshoppers on the farm. Those spit brown water, called tobacco, and they made tasty snack for chickens.

'That was the only reason to like them,' thought Anthony, 'these are big, they could hurt me. Thinking about grasshoppers makes me hungry.' "Maybe the grocery store is open." Anthony said the last sentence aloud to himself. He was hungry, he watched the big metal grasshoppers, they hadn't moved so far so maybe they won't.

Anthony went into the grocery store. It didn't look like any grocery store that he'd seen. He had looked through a window at a store back in Pettigrew it didn't look like this one. He saw a lot of shelves, being a small chicken he

couldn't see anything on the high shelves. On some of the shelves were many cans of corn, tomatoes, carrots and beans. There were cans of coffee, crackers and laundry soap. He saw small boxes of jello too. On the other side of the store were more shelves. They held candy, toys, fabric, shoes, dishes, tools and twine. There were big sacks of potatoes and flour by the door. As Anthony walked along the floor he saw a big, black, cast iron stove in the center for heat probably. In the back was a post office and a place where the meat was cut. Further back was the family living quarters. Anthony walked back to where the cans were. He accidentally knocked a few off the shelf and discovered they were empty! None of the food was real! The apples the oranges and the grapes all had a plastic shine to them.

"I'm hungry," said Anthony, "what am I suppose to do now?"

The bugs, gravel and leaves looked pretty good now. He walked out the screen door and sat on the bench in front of the grocery store. He looked down the boardwalk, he saw the Doctor's Office and the Print Shop, he knew there wasn't any food there. So Anthony sat on the bench thinking about what to do next. Then the cat walked by the tree. Anthony stiffened, he didn't want the cat to see him. The cat raised her head and sniffed the air. She saw that there was something different at the Grocery Store. She wanted to know what it was. The cat thought she smelled a chicken. Anthony the Chicken wished at that moment he was invisible. He stiffened his body as much as he could. Perhaps the cat would think he was a statue. Then the cat saw him.

The cat began whispering, 'Don't worry, my name is Isabel, I just want to talk. Earlier someone didn't finish their food so they threw it away! I ate it! Since I just ate I'm not hungry.' Isabel was sure she hadn't seen chickens at the museum before.

Anthony wasn't sure if he should trust the cat but what choice did he have. Now Isabel was walking slowly towards him. She probably knew by now that he wasn't a statue. Anthony looked at Isabel, by now she had sat down on the grass looking at him.

Isabel reassured Anthony again, "Remember I've already eaten, I'm not hungry, believe me. What's your name?"

Anthony started to relax, he began to believe Isabel. "Anthony the chicken. Where am I? Nothing's real here," asked Anthony.

"You're at a museum. They show people what is was like here in the 1920's and 30's."

"I'm awfully hungry. Is there anything around here to eat?"

"Not unless there's some kind of special event going on. Then I hide," answered Isabel.

"Nothing at all," said Anthony.

Isabel thought a moment then said, "Every morning the caretaker puts out food for me at the door of the shop."

"Is some still there?" asked Anthony, "All this talk about food has made me hungry."

"Do you like dry food? That's what he usually puts out," said Isabel "because I nibble off and on all day."

"That's fine, dry cat food I hope. I don't like dog food. Show me, where's the shop?"

Isabel pointed with her tail then she said, "It's across the yard by that big gray building next to the wooden one. He always puts the food in a bowl on a mat outside the front door. There's oil and gas signs on the wall on the outside."

"Thanks for telling me and showing me," said Anthony.

Anthony waved at Isabel and started walking in the direction of the gray building. He tried to keep an eye on those big metal grasshoppers. Actually there were only three big ones and three smaller ones. The small ones were still bigger than the ones on the farm. They still hadn't moved.

'What are they called, oh yeah pump jacks, there's a cannon. Why would a cannon be in an oil field?' thought Anthony.

Anthony saw next to it was a sign but he was to hungry. He'd read it after he'd eaten. As a chicken he took smaller steps to get to the shop so it took him longer. There was the food! Where Isabel said it would be. His hat had stayed on his head, he reached up to feel it to be sure. A small metal bowl was on top of an old rug. He had never felt so hungry.

The dry cat food bits were smaller but he still needed to break them with a rock. They tasted much better that the dog food.

'Almost anything would be better than dog food,' Anthony made a face.

He was chewing and he turned to look at the cannon. He looked back at his bowl.

He swallowed and thought, "I need to remember to back and learn why a cannon is in an oil field." He looked around. "Where did Isabel go? After all Isabel was still a cat. I'm still a bird. Even if Isabel was helpful she was still a cat."

While Anthony was chewing he kept an eye out for Isabel. Then he saw Isabel walking up to him.

"Great you found the food. Does it taste alright?" Isabel asked.

"It hits the spot," answered Anthony.

"By the way." Isabel asked as she sat down, "What made you stop at a museum?"

Anthony finished the bowl. "Thanks for the food," he said. "Well I was wanting to learn how to drill for oil. I wanted an adventure so I hopped on an empty train car, then I saw all this," Anthony as he waved his feather over the small buildings.

"You rode a train here? That would be an adventure for me" said Isabel.

"It was wonderful," continued Anthony, "anyway this town looked like a nice place. I figured I could learn how to dig for oil here. But nothing is real and usable here."

"I know," said Isabel, "it's like I told you. This is a pretend town like in the 1920's and 30's. You found out. There's no real food in the grocery store. You staying here tonight?"

"Yeah, probably at the wash house that place worked well last night."

"Great, come see the rest of the museum."

"The rest of it? There's more?"

"Of course! There's lots to see here. The Power House, the Cable Tool Rig, the Lease House and more. Over that way," Isabel pointed.

Anthony saw the tops of the oil derricks, they were tall. To tall for a chicken. "Will I be be able to dig for oil?" he asked.

"At least you'll learn how it used to be done," said Isabel.

"H-m-m-m maybe I'll get an idea," said Anthony.

"Maybe," said Isabel and she nodded.

Anthony the Chicken had a lot of time so he walked to the small wooden building. He looked inside and saw that there were just different kinds of machinery in it. There was a small wooden sidewalk to the large building. He read the sign in front and inside was the Cable Tool Rig. Since Isabel had mentioned one he wanted to see inside. Anthony walked inside and there was a big area with no windows. He looked down, in the floor was a large hole with the big Cable Tool rig in it.

"I suppose it just pounded and pounded the ground until the ground split apart," thought Anthony. He looked down and wondered "It's awfully deep, if I got down there I'd never be able to get out!"

Anthony looked around and saw where he wanted to be, "There a lazy bench would be for me! Except I wouldn't sleep there. I'd just roost there and watch the other workers." He saw two metal teapots, each one with two spouts. There was one on the floor, "I'll need to ask Isabel about those," he thought.

He looked around some more and saw some big pulleys in the middle of the room. Anthony guessed they were at least ten chickens tall.

Anthony walked out the same door he had entered and next to the building was a tool rack. All the tools seemed big and heavy.

"It would take at least six chickens to lift those," he thought when he saw them.

Straight ahead on the same wooden boardwalk was another oil derrick. A red one. Anthony read a sign that said it was a Spudder.

"So this is what was used to drill for oil," he said to himself.

Anthony looked up and up. There was a ladder made of separate 'U-shaped' metal rods attached to the side.

"WOW! I'm sure that someone climbed up there but not me. Chickens can't even fly that high," said Anthony out loud.

Near the Spudder the sidewalk led in another direction. A concrete sidewalk went to the Lease House.

"Now that's where I need to go," he said, "Look there's a little gray house behind it."

He walked down the sidewalk and up the steps to the Lease House. He noticed behind the screen the wooden door was open. Anthony opened the screen door and walked inside. In the front room on one side Anthony saw a small bed with a quilt on top. On the other side was a sewing machine, a rocking chair, a radio (that didn't work) and two small chairs. There was a rug on the floor and on that rug were some toys.

"Boy if I left anything on the floor of the chicken coop I'd be in trouble, especially if I left my hat," thought Anthony.

He felt it on his head. The sewing machine was by the window. He saw the sunlight pour through the open curtains. There were two windows and pictures on the walls and a blue barrier. It was like a fence Anthony couldn't get to the rest of the house. He saw a plastic paper in a wooden pocket on the top of the barrier. He wanted to know what was printed on it so he jumped onto the small table then on to the top of the barrier. He walked over the top to the wooden pocket. He pulled out the plastic paper with his beak, He held it between his feathers and he read what was inside the house. This was an actual shot-gun house. A person could see directly from one end of the house to the other. That's what makes a shot-gun house.

'Oh like the trailer, where I could sit on a chair and see the whole trailer,' remembered Anthony.

Anthony kept reading and read that in an oil town no out buildings like sheds or chicken coops were permitted.

"No chicken coops, that's not very nice," he said out loud to no one in particular.

He looked up and saw the rest of the house. The kitchen was the farthest back so Anthony couldn't see very much of it. The middle room looked like the bedroom. In it was a double bed with a quilt on it, there was a crib next to it. Across the room was the dresser with a mirror on it. He looked, saw that his hat was till on his head and his lucky feather was still in the brim. Near the dresser was an iron stove like the one he had seen in the grocery store but not as fancy. Long underwear was hanging from an inside clothesline over the iron stove. A stack of wood was ready next to the stove. There were also a comb, brush and a hand mirror on top of the dresser. There were baby toys in the crib, behind the crib was a small closet.

"That small closet would be just the right size for me. I don't have any clothes. Except for my hat." Anthony said.

He looked some more, he was sad he couldn't see the rest of the house. He jumped from the barrier to the small bed then to the floor. Anthony walked across the porch. There was so much more to see at this museum. Some of the machinery he saw from the porch was probably antique. Anthony saw another oil rig, a very tall one. There was a sign reading that this was a Rotary Rig.

'It's still very tall,' thought Anthony.

There was another derrick and at the top of that derrick was an American Flag. South of the oil derrick was a row of gas stations signs, Conoco, Standard, Sinclair Anthony recognized some of the names, there were almost twenty of them. He'd seen a building called a Power Unit, it's metal doors were closed. Anthony followed the side walk back to the metal grasshoppers. They still hadn't moved.

"It doesn't matter what their real name is they look like big metal grasshoppers to me," thought Anthony as he watched them. There was a railroad car behind the grocery store. He read that it was used to haul the crude oil to the refinery. He saw Isabel walking to him. Anthony had stiffened out of habit, he'd learned he didn't need to be afraid of Isabel.

She spoke first, "You got any questions for me? I've been here a long time."

"Oh yeah, what was the cannon used for," said Anthony

"I hear that a lot," said Isabel. "It was used to put out tank fires. See...it's pointing towards the tanks."

Anthony spoke first, "This was some museum! I didn't even go inside the building."

"I knew you'd like it," said Isabel, "but you should've gone inside."

"I don't think anyone would've liked seeing a chicken indoors."

"Maybe," Isabel said and shook her head and shrugged her shoulders.

"Who knew that one of my friends on this adventure would be a cat!"

"Yeah I suppose but I am glad we met."

"So am I."

"Come back when you can. See the inside," said Isabel.

"I'm not sure when that will be. Maybe on my next adventure," said Anthony.

"When's your next adventure," asked Isabel.

"I'm not sure Isabel I'll think about it when I get back to my farm in Pettigrew."

"Good-bye, have a safe trip."

"Bye Isabel. I've got my lucky hat with a feather in it. It was nice to meet you," Anthony pointed to his hat on his head and started walking back to the train tracks.

"Now this was some adventure. I can hardly wait to tell Bugger and Dick the refrigerator all about it. I'll need to tell Dick I met his critter's cousin named Rex," said Anthony to himself.

He walked in the direction of the schoolhouse. While he was waiting for a train he thought about his new friend Isabel. "Who would believe that my best friend on this adventure was a cat! Certainly not Bugger he never felt that cats were worth very much anyway."

This story was inspired by my volunteer work at the Kansas Oil Museum in El Dorado, KS. I give them my thanks! Thank-you! Thank-you!

10620 Treena Street, Suite 230
San Diego, California,
CA 92131 USA
www.readersmagnet.com
1.619.354.2643
Copyright 2022 All Rights Reserved

www.ingramcontent.com/pod-product-compliance
Lightning Source LLC
LaVergne TN
LVHW020135080526
838202LV00047B/3947